SILENT ANATO

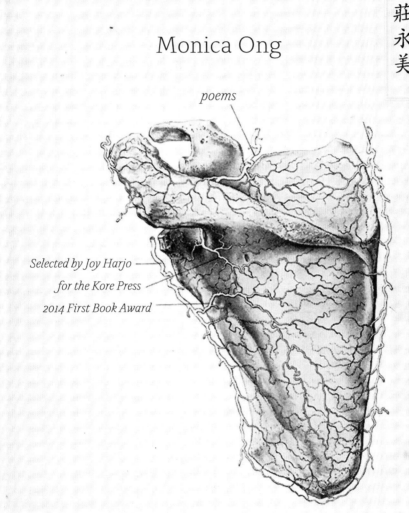

Monica Ong

poems

莊
永
美

Selected by Joy Harjo
for the Kore Press
2014 First Book Award

KORE PRESS · TUCSON · 2015

Kore Press, Inc., Tucson, Arizona USA
Standing by women's words since 1993
www.korepress.org

Lines from "Action and Non-Action" by Chuang Tzu translated by Thomas Merton, from
The Way of Chuang Tzu, copyright ©1965 by The Abbey of Gethsemani. Reprinted by
permission of New Directions Publishing Corp.

Cover art and design by Monica Ong
Typographic design collaboration by Sally Geier, Lisa Bowden, and Monica Ong
Text set in Alda, an original typeface designed by Berton Hasebe in 2008

We express gratitude for individual gifts, especially from Helen Schaefer and Eva Harris,
and for partial support from the National Endowment for the Arts.

ISBN: 978-1-888553-69-7

CIP data is available for this book

I wish I could tenderly lift from the dark side of history, voices that are anonymous, slighted—inarticulate.

–Susan Howe

2018

Table of Contents

THE GLASS LARYNX.

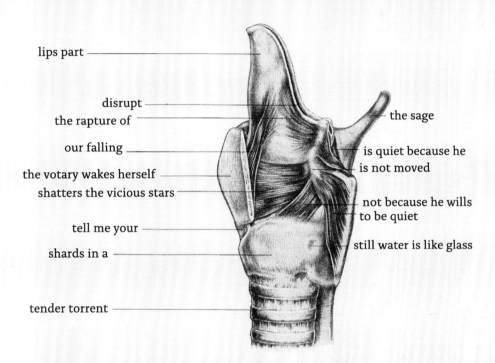

lips part

disrupt
the rapture of

our falling

the votary wakes herself

shatters the vicious stars

tell me your

shards in a

tender torrent

the sage

is quiet because he
is not moved

not because he wills
to be quiet

still water is like glass

Right side is from "Action and Non-Action" by Chuang Tzu

MEDICA V. CHUANG TZU

BO SUERTE

Mother, each day I look for you. Try to recognize you in soup and sepia.
As it happens in other lives, you come to me in secret.
There were no elegant stairs in your childhood home, and this young woman, the nanny.
Just the way her brows bend with humidity.

I easily identify all four of your sisters in their von Trapp dresses,
and both brothers, sporting crisp white linen.
In your absence stands a son, slightly leaning, toes
ablister from your brother's too big shoes.

You tell me Grandfather was ashamed.
He didn't want people shaking their heads, their tongues clicking:
Bo suerte.

Bo, which in Hokkien means *without*, or *not enough*.
It does explain the hoarding, I suppose. Dusty magazines stacked into pillars.
Grandmother's purse of purloined sporks.
The way your long locks fell like black feathers onto the kitchen floor.

Suerte, is Catholic for *karma*, cruel as hunger, heavy as stone.
The fact of five daughters was the immutable kind.
Payback, perhaps, for an unsavory ancestor in an imperial court?
Or something during the war that Grandfather never told us?

Hidden like your graceful arms in a brother's long sleeves.
Your boyface gazes at me. I place flowers at your feet, wet with pus.
For the daughter, you, but not only you.

Portrait as battle. The terror of asymmetry. This shortage of sons.

PAPER SON
On the Origin of Ong

The eye of occupation closed on the island. Its name Xiamen means *lower gate*. In 1938 the diaspora unfurled from a seaport hemorrhage. Father's father left little detail about the crossing. What can be salvaged from blackened memory? On the other shore, the landing in Luzon was another kind of founding. *Foundling.*

It was not uncommon to purchase papers bearing the names of the dead. *Ong* was the ghost that carried him. Name as shelter. Name as shell, washed up on the jungle's edge. Verification did not require photos, so he got by on approximate age. Such soft cocoons would shepherd kin who blended, barefoot, into the barrios.

By 1941, the second eye came closing. Imagine mapping births around aerial bombs. Manila, then Malabon, then hurriedly on to San Juan. This name pregnant from war, moving, always moving, around a rubbled bay held captive. Beneath the flag of the rising sun, his was considered the lesser invasion.

Name less alien. The sweaty streets call out *Intsik!* His pith grew pungent with the kalamansi rinds, curled beneath the kitchen altar. Home was a door to take off one's shoes, to unload the brickbats still burning beside them. Name within windows, he remained *Cheng* in the Hokkien home, or *Chuang* its Mandarin twin, chewing on cigarettes at the table with sleight of mahjong hand. Sometimes the swallow longs for his mother's music.

One time the *pulis* picked him out, citing a jar of ink, priced five cents too high. As though for fun, they threw Grandpa in the military prison. *For a week?* I ask father. *No, for one year.* The ghost returned to give lessons on the incognito arts.

Name of the Asunción. Name after San Pedro, holy holy. Name in search of Vicente. Name for Elena, the bright one. Name as Marieta, the shadow. Name in the distance, Alejandro.

He recited them all, his children's faces.

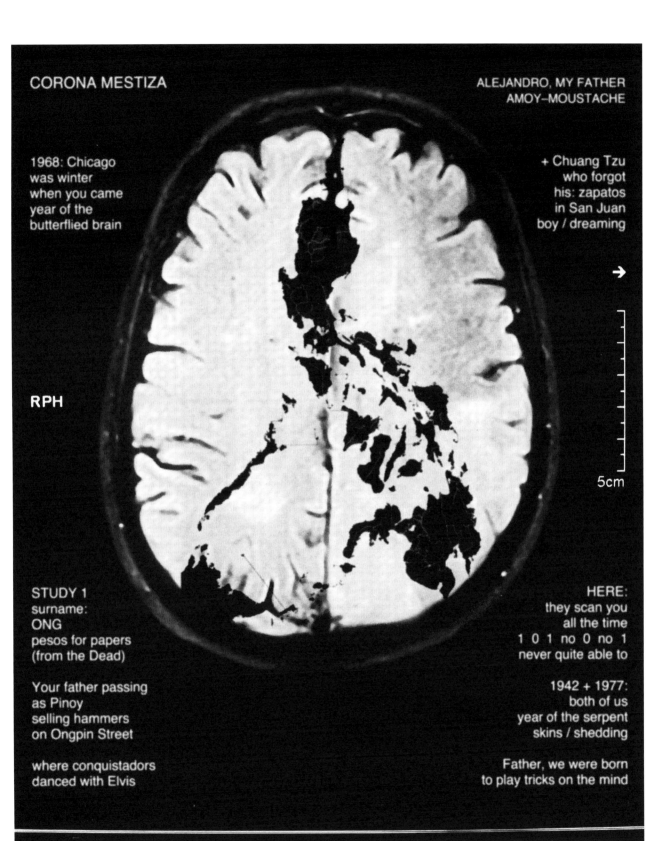

CORONA MESTIZA

ALEJANDRO, MY FATHER
AMOY–MOUSTACHE

1968: Chicago
was winter
when you came
year of the
butterflied brain

+ Chuang Tzu
who forgot
his: zapatos
in San Juan
boy / dreaming

→

5cm

RPH

STUDY 1
surname:
ONG
pesos for papers
(from the Dead)

Your father passing
as Pinoy
selling hammers
on Ongpin Street

where conquistadors
danced with Elvis

HERE:
they scan you
all the time
1 0 1 no 0 no 1
never quite able to

1942 + 1977:
both of us
year of the serpent
skins / shedding

Father, we were born
to play tricks on the mind

FORTUNE BABIES

DIRECTIONS

If you have difficulty conceiving, adopt a little boy so that spirits fill your home with blessings for many sons. Grandma showed results within weeks of adopting Se-Ahn. I had never heard of my Mystery Uncle until this picture inside my mother's cookbook. *While playing outside I fell on my wrist - and they would not take me to the doctor.* He recalls the dull pain, his bloodless lineage. A small bone out of place beneath the flesh. Still, mother calls him Big Brother.

CAUTION: Does not guarantee protection from bearing daughters. Consult your fortune teller if you suspect your pregnancy may be at risk.

ANCIENT CHINESE SECRET

FORTUNE BABIES

DIRECTIONS

If you have difficulty conceiving, adopt a little boy so that spirits fill your home with blessings for many sons. Grandma showed results within weeks of adopting Se-Ahn. I had never heard of my Mystery Uncle until this picture inside my mother's cookbook. *While playing outside I fell on my wrist—and they would not take me to the doctor.* He recalls the dull pain, his bloodless lineage. A small bone out of place beneath the flesh. Still, mother calls him Big Brother.

CAUTION: Does not guarantee protection from bearing daughters. Consult your fortune teller if you suspect your pregnancy may be at risk.

CATCHING A WAVE

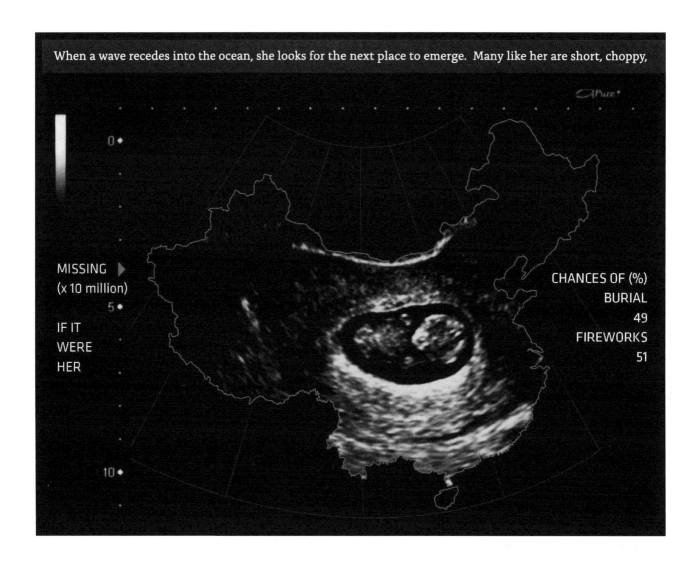

When a wave recedes into the ocean, she looks for the next place to emerge. Many like her are short, choppy,

MISSING ▶
(x 10 million)

IF IT
WERE
HER

CHANCES OF (%)
BURIAL
49
FIREWORKS
51

smashed into rocks. Obliterated. She longs for a willful tide that could see her through an entire lifespan.

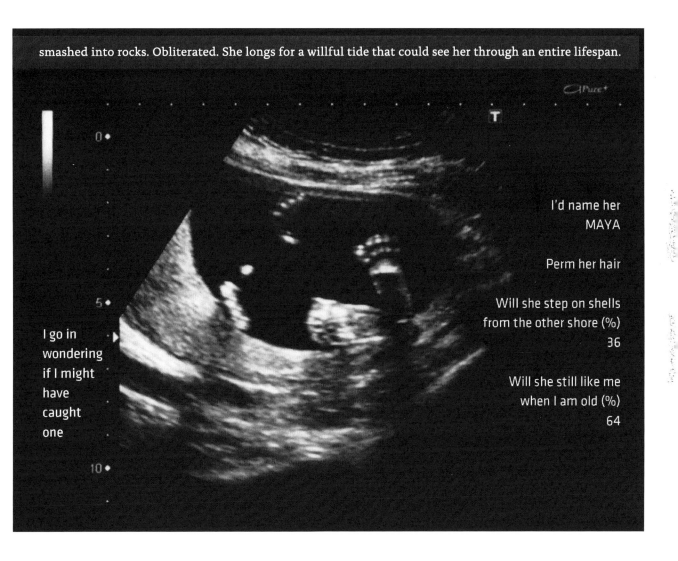

I'd name her
MAYA

Perm her hair

Will she step on shells
from the other shore (%)
36

Will she still like me
when I am old (%)
64

I go in
wondering
if I might
have
caught
one

I want to know so I can coordinate her nursery to pantone perfection, pick out toys, our matching dresses.

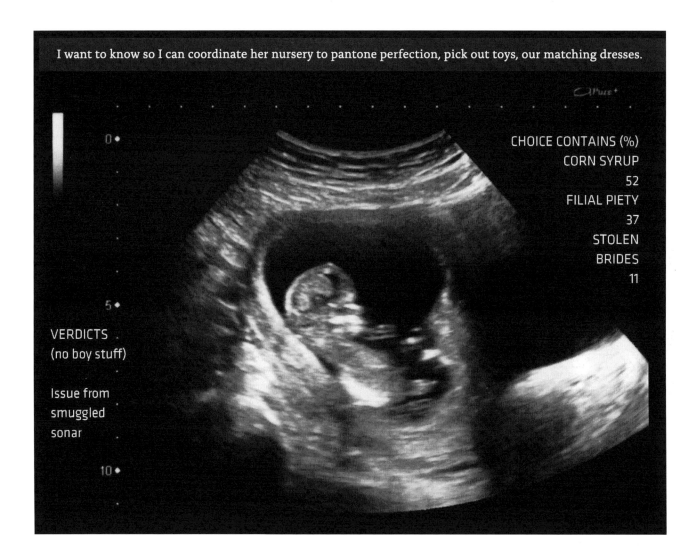

CHOICE CONTAINS (%)
CORN SYRUP
52
FILIAL PIETY
37
STOLEN
BRIDES
11

VERDICTS
(no boy stuff)

Issue from
smuggled
sonar

Somewhere a line, fractures between us. Bloodshot. From the hemisphere where cliffs narrow to a pointed ledge.

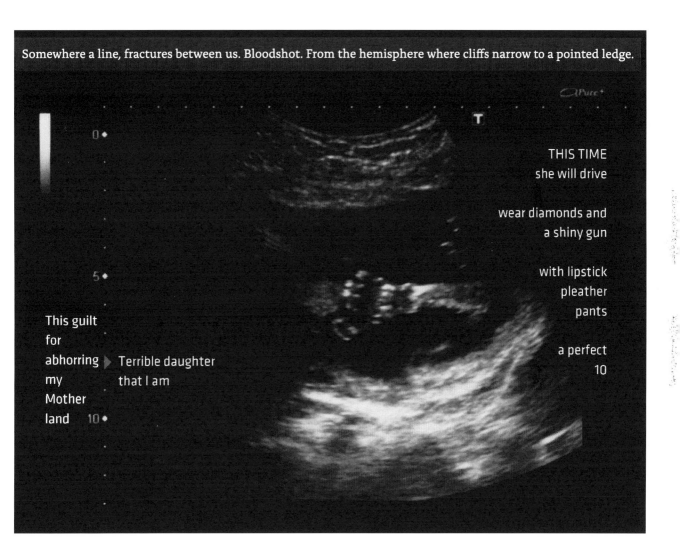

THIS TIME
she will drive

wear diamonds and
a shiny gun

with lipstick
pleather
pants

This guilt
for
abhorring ▶ Terrible daughter
my   that I am
Mother
land

a perfect
10

Will she rely on echoes to find her way home, smell me in the waters as I unfurl my dark floor, close my eyes to cast

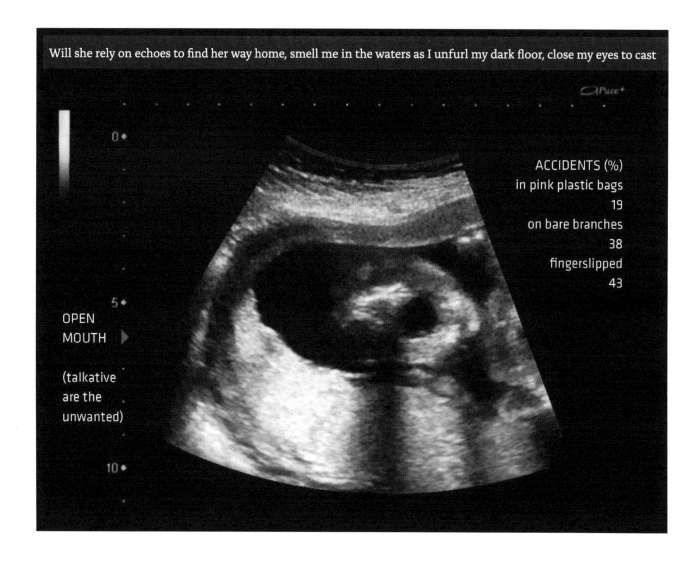

out wide nets? What is the danger in this kind of wishing, of sitting like an empty well beneath overgrown grasses?

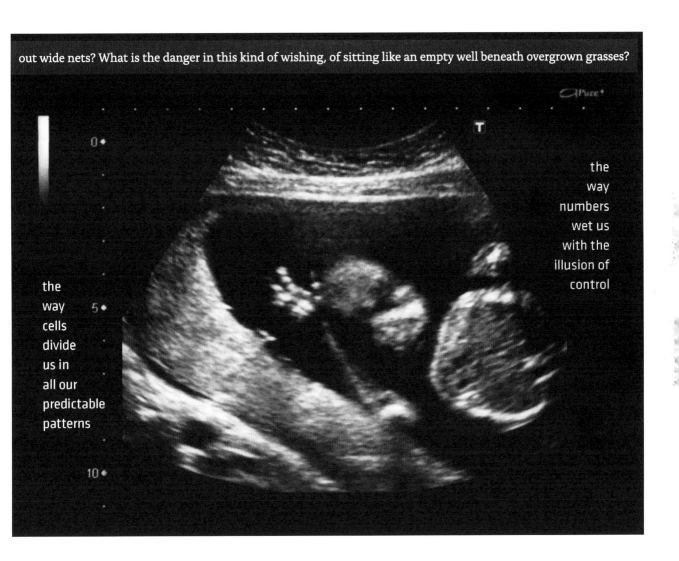

the
way
cells
divide
us in
all our
predictable
patterns

the
way
numbers
wet us
with the
illusion of
control

PERFECT
BABY FORMULA

WHY SETTLE?

Indicated for pregnant women to curb the onset of physiological and psychosocial deficiencies in early fetal development. Gender correction treatment promotes production of the anti-Mullerian hormone (AMH), testosterone and dihydrotestosterone, which promote fetal masculinization. Also proven efficacy for superior academic performance leading to professional overachievement. Prevents homosexual tendencies.

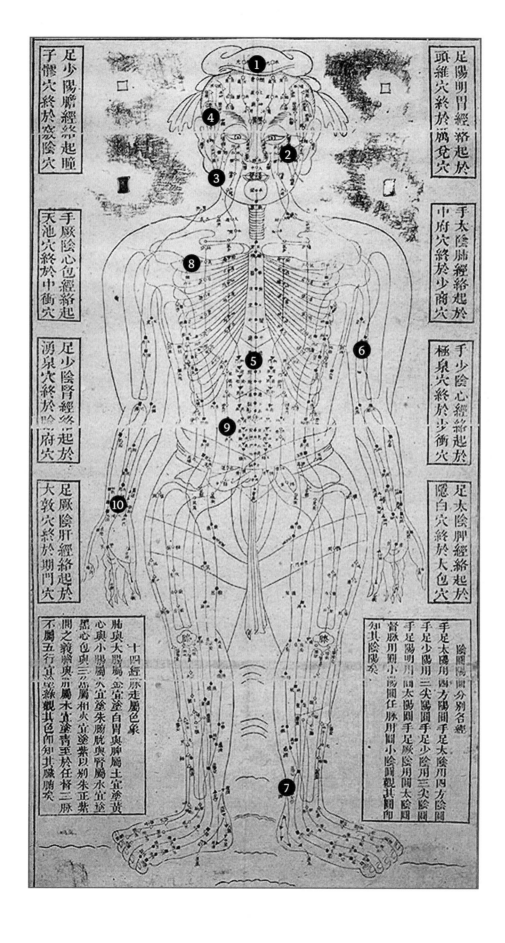

足少陽膽經絡起於
子髎穴終於竅陰穴

足陽明胃經絡起於
頭維穴終於厲兌穴

手厥陰心包經絡起
天池穴終於中衝穴

手太陰肺經絡起於
中府穴終於少商穴

足少陰腎經絡終起於
湧泉穴終於陰府穴

手少陰心經絡起於
極泉穴終於少衝穴

足厥陰肝經絡起於
大敦穴終於期門穴

足太陰脾經絡起於
隱白穴終於大包穴

子髎穴終於任督二脉
肺與大腸屬金宜塗白胃與脾屬土宜塗黃
心與小腸屬火宜塗朱膀胱與腎屬水宜塗
墨心包與三焦屬相火宜塗紫以別朱正紫
聞之義紫與心焦屬水宜塗青至於任督二脉
不屬五行宜寫綠觀其色即知其臟腑矣

十四經原走屬色象

陰陽陽明分別名經
手足太陽用圓方陽開手足太陰用四方陰開
手足少陽用三尖陽開手足少陰用三尖陰開
手足陽明用圓太陽開手足厥陰開太陰開
腎脉用圓小腸開任脉用圓小腸開觀其開闔
知其陰陽矣

MEDICA VISITS *the* WITCH DOCTOR

1. Dear Witch Doctor—I have brought you a bag of rice, two unmarried cousins, and a stone in a glass of water. Despite miles of oppressive heat, I have walked here in my new *tsinelas*. Let us commence this ceremony with an egg.

2. Begin with the thumbs below the cheekbones. This will clear the sinuses of guilty pleasures: Espresso grinds that feed the cankers. Gossip masked by orange peels. The way I follow the cologne of old men from the crosswalk, closely behind. No more touching below, no more scent of honey or buzzing bees.

3. You promised me skin that lusters with heavenly beauty, red empress curls and one less chin. Take my moles, my capillary lines. Make it straight. Make me light. Magic incisions, round my eyes.

4. Place your fingertips on my temples. I like that they are round and cold. Conjuring grandma's cypress shadow that tends to visit in the night. Her bony fingers tremble from crown to pillow checking, only to find damp hair. She scolds me, warns that I shall wake up blind.

5. Slather me, work the mix of golden yolks deep into my spine. Right there. This is where I left my tunes, the piano I once played. Nothing but unrepressed laughter. Before the bottle, I was a boat with tall white sails.

6. Move slowly along the lung meridian, to the block where the winters are long. You will need to push quite hard to release these ghost contractions, the scarlet sheets, and that morning's soft snow impressed with a single angel.

7. This point is not as forgiving. The consequence of getting on the express train. Without him.

8. My regrets are tucked inside the scapula. Go there, I need you to stay awhile. Don't cut yourself in the shipwreck, or get pricked by all my splinters. I buried a corpse there once, a girl I used to inhabit. She was always pressed for time.

9. This is where the phone went dead. When a *mangkukulam* possessed my sister and cast me from her driveway. But I do not miss her, not at all. I am crying because my liver is on fire. A little more pressure please. I need her rain.

10. Press here to untangle the north wind, whose kite tail flutters from a canopy of bronchial trees. Flight can be fragile, bungled by words. Everything I wish I had never said: knots. You may need to use your knuckles.

Yeong 永　Mae's 美

WHITENING SOLUTION

"IF YOU HAVE WHITE SKIN
YOU CAN COVER 1,000 UGLINESSES."
- *Chinese Proverb*

TO USE: Apply liberally to clean face and body daily.
Our patented triple-whitening complex is formulated
with tyrosinase enzymes to stop hyperpigmentation.
Infused kojic acid neutralizes facial hair and other
ethnic features. Also contains glutathione to even out
blemishes such as freckles, scars, and birthmarks.

With the help of exfoliation agents, the initial effects of
this complex can be seen within three weeks. Studies
have shown efficacy in elevating social standing, while
lowering incidents of racial profiling by 27%. Pooled
analyses of single females who have undergone this
whitening treatment reveal a 45% higher success rate
in securing marriage proposals.

Try together with Yeong Mae's Whitening Oral Rinse

AS ANCIENT CHINESE SECRET SA

WHITENING SOLUTION

If you have white skin you can cover 1,000 uglinesses.
–Chinese Proverb

TO USE: Apply liberally to clean face and body daily. Our patented triple-whitening complex is formulated with tyrosinase enzymes to stop hyperpigmentation. Infused kojic acid neutralizes facial hair and other ethnic features. Also contains glutathione to even out blemishes such as freckles, scars, and birthmarks.

With the help of exfoliation agents, the initial effects of this complex can be seen within three weeks. Studies have shown efficacy in elevating social standing, while lowering incidents of racial profiling by 27%. Pooled analysis of single females who have undergone this whitening treatment reveal a 45% higher success rate in securing marriage proposals.

Try together with Yeong Mae's Oral Whitening Rinse

ORAL WHITENING RINSE

Beautiful words are not truthful, the truth is not beautiful.
–Chinese Paradox

LOSE YOUR ACCENT IN 30 DAYS—GUARANTEED
Antiseptic rinse kills 99% of all loose terms and fights slang build-up. Patented accent reduction treatment also eliminates stains and bad breath. Swish in mouth undiluted for 30 seconds, then spit out. Use daily after breakfast and before bedtime.

Our gentle Lingo-ease formula relaxes the mother tongue, naturalizing muscles with significant syllable stress. Leaves mouth fresh and minty cool. Dynamic foaming action noticeably whitens speech.

Studies have shown that consistent use over a period of four weeks can dramatically improve one's chances of becoming articulate—Results may vary.

Try together with Yeong Mae's Whitening Solution

METAL LUNGS.

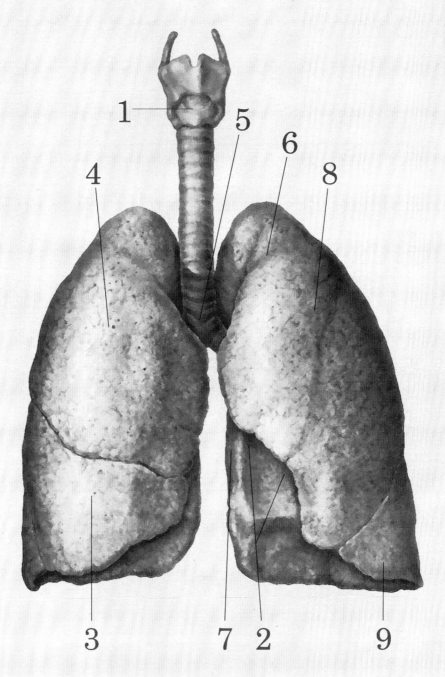

ANTERIOR VIEW OF TRACHEA AND LUNGS

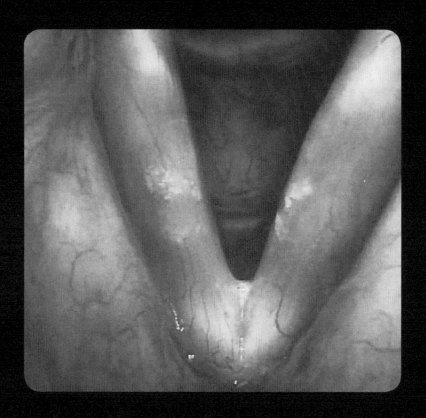

1   Walking membranes we
guard the gateway flux of
breath (his) coming in
and the *po* spirits pushing out
past moistened boundaries
discomfort unclaimed
by an eager glottis

2   You could say the wind
had been knocked out of her—
black tangle in his thick fingers
that snap her head off the
click click burner as
he stoops down to light
a lucky strike

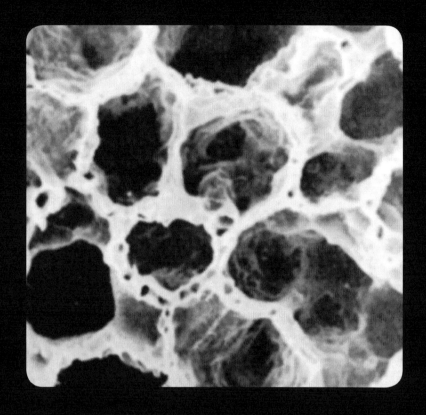

3   Breath (hers) never quite leaves the body,
but recedes into *qi*
native to the lungs
then gathers, searches for coordinates
mapping a red line across the border—
oxygen soldiers huddle in the
flora alveoli
quivering beneath the ribs
summoning a call to action

4   Morning, however, is a long exhale—

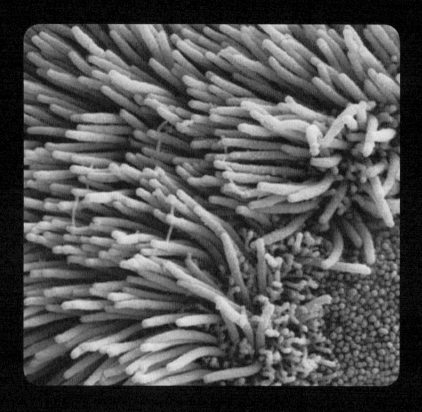

5   The uncounted testimonies
tethered in the trachea
where daughters (we)
are trained
to exchange melancholia for metal:
braces hugged by yellow cankers
razors that carve pink release beneath the sleeve
the smooth armor of anonymity

6   [And who in this white cube
     can decipher the endangered dialect
     thinning in her throat?]

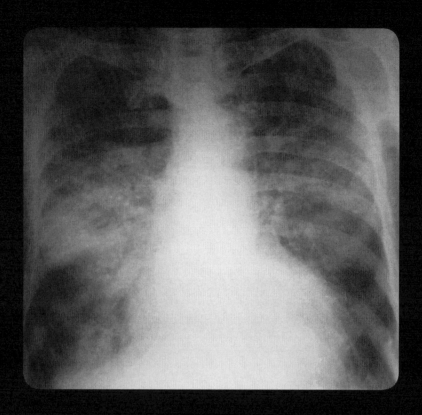

7   *True breath has its origin in the heart.*
In my sleep I am wandering sidewalk smog
out of the gray cloud billowing,
fist and fissure
secreting names
faces
(hers, her mother's, and yes,
her daughter's too)

8   *It is rude to finish other people's sentences.*
     I have been warned
     but my ribcage keeps expanding
     this hoarder rummaging through
     auto wreckages
     scouring scrap and hinge
     anything bent beyond repair
     until all my capillaries
     cry *Uncle!*

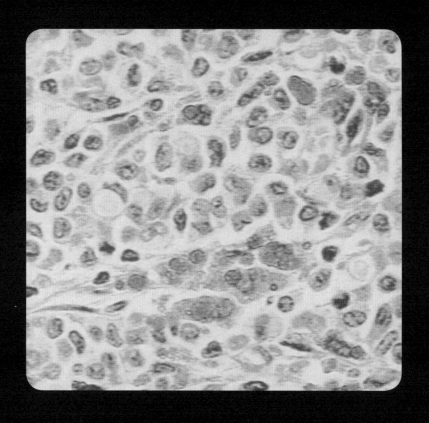

9   If we knew all the floods
     that get trapped in the lungs

INNERVATION.

1. Deep in the interior division, Mother's words nest:
2. *One eye open, one eye closed.* (Because I am raw,
3. All red inside.) Shame as communicans.
4. We open up on each other's walls. Sympathetic,
5. But never in the same room.
6. *Blood is thicker than water.* I waited for her. Still do.
7. There is a way to cultivate birds from torn things,
8. Find oceans in empty seats, her heavy door. How
9. Do her words weigh on these muscular branches?
10. *You have to collect and select.* Cutaneous gall.
11. Tiny hands cup sand and blue sea glass.
12. Anterior to the outbreak of war. Yet—
13. We sleep best under each other's skin.

DIARY OF AN INTERCOASTAL NERVE

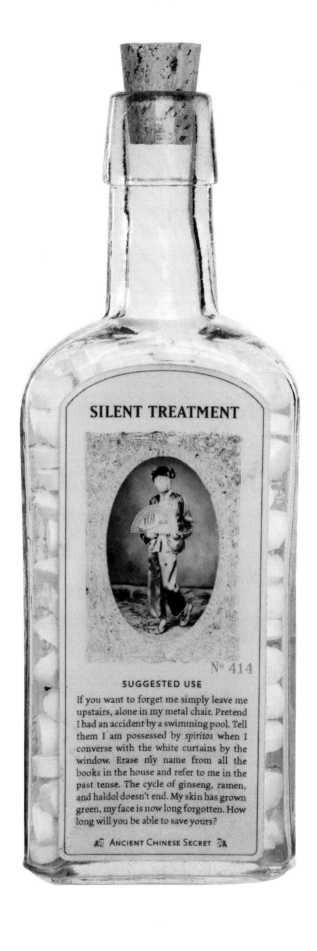

SILENT TREATMENT

№ 414

SUGGESTED USE

If you want to forget me simply leave me upstairs, alone in my metal chair. Pretend I had an accident by a swimming pool. Tell them I am possessed by *spiritos* when I converse with the white curtains by the window. Erase my name from all the books in the house and refer to me in the past tense. The cycle of ginseng, ramen, and haldol doesn't end. My skin has grown green, my face is now long forgotten. How long will you be able to save yours?

ANCIENT CHINESE SECRET

SILENT TREATMENT

SUGGESTED USE

If you want to forget me simply leave me upstairs, alone in my metal chair. Pretend I had an accident by a swimming pool. Tell them I am possessed by *spiritos* when I converse with the white curtains by the window. Erase my name from all the books in the house and refer to me in the past tense. The cycle of ginseng, ramen, and haldol doesn't end. My skin has grown green, my face is now long forgotten. How long will you be able to save yours?

HER YOUTH IN ASIA

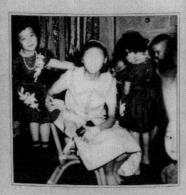

The ghosts laughing upstairs (see *delusions*) make her clench her fists in long, dull silences (see *alogia*). Doctors didn't know *spiritos* entered Auntie's body during her youth, and lured her mind into an endless dream.

USE AS DIRECTED: *If this ever happens to me, please give me pills so I can fall asleep and wake in heaven,* Mother sighs, when she looks into her sister's vacant eyes (see *catatonia*). Are we all just in a dream, trying to wake up?

ANCIENT CHINESE SECRET

HER YOUTH IN ASIA

The ghosts laughing upstairs (see *delusions*) make her clench her fists in long, dull silences (see *alogia*). Doctors didn't know *spiritos* entered Auntie's body during her youth, and lured her mind into an endless dream.

USE AS DIRECTED: *If this ever happens to me, please give me pills so I can fall asleep and wake in heaven,* Mother sighs when she looks into her sister's vacant eyes (see *catatonia*). Are we all just in a dream, trying to wake up?

ETYMOLOGY *of an* UNTRANSLATED CERVIX

In Rufumbira, the local language here in Kisoro, there is no word for cervix,
and the word vagina is a shameful, dirty word, rarely uttered. —Erin Cox, MD

This space between two entries
I claim it.

When it (she) is blotted out with black marker
I say it, I name it.

But under these volcano peaks, I am locked out in English.

Cells rupture. Quietly.
A carcinoma colony creeping in her blank space. Spreads.

What if *dysplasia* simply meant
to displease?

The interpreter asks

Why do they want to go *down there,*
to that dirty, shameful place?

What is the point of wailing horns, of fighting
a fire with no address?

This dialect was not designed for *her*.

On the Western shore, I can spell it out, letter by letter
print a scan and map every tumor's point of entry,

conduct daily surveillance on each tendril
until it is white with radioactive surge.

But what about *her* tongue?

Absent, unable to make real
her body, written in silence.

Danger: (   ) is waiting in red,
The monster's shadow, taller and hungrier than the monster itself.

Ink spilled. Bleeding.

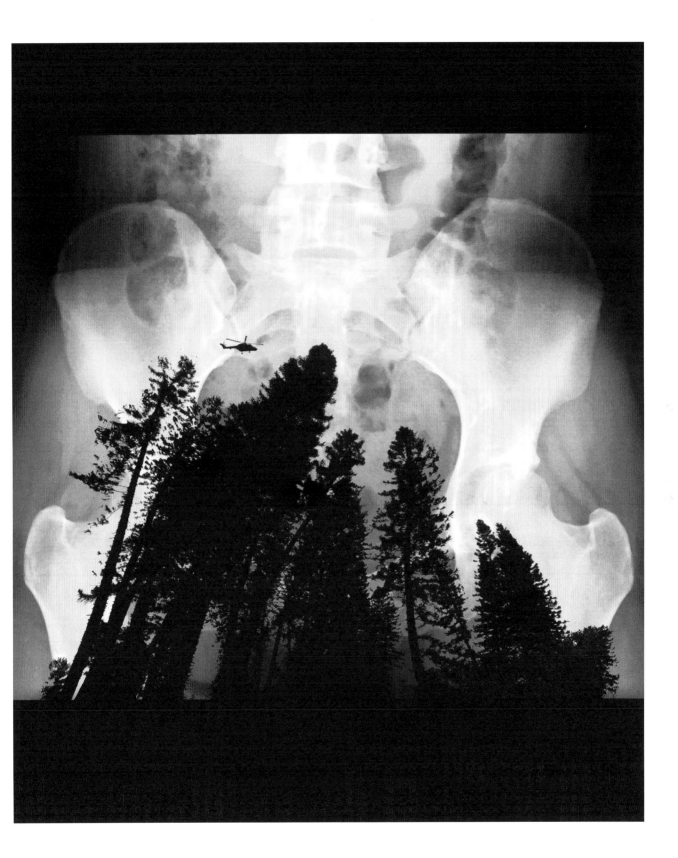

ELEGY.

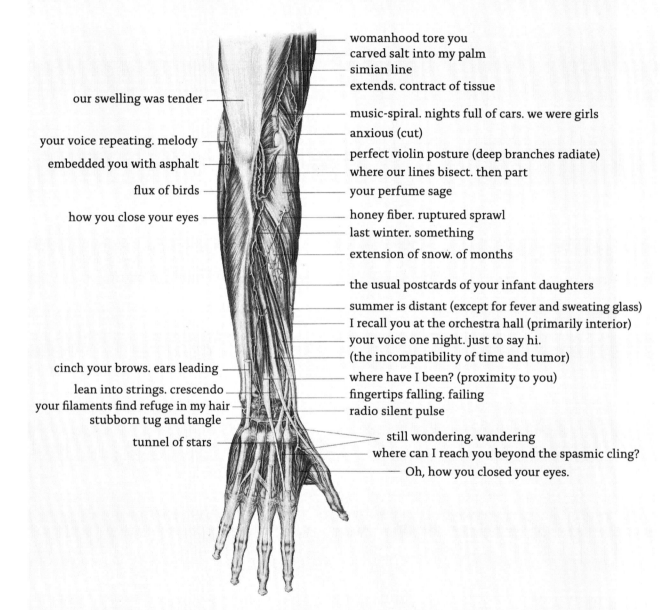

our swelling was tender

your voice repeating. melody

embedded you with asphalt

flux of birds

how you close your eyes

cinch your brows. ears leading

lean into strings. crescendo

your filaments find refuge in my hair

stubborn tug and tangle

tunnel of stars

womanhood tore you

carved salt into my palm

simian line

extends. contract of tissue

music-spiral. nights full of cars. we were girls

anxious (cut)

perfect violin posture (deep branches radiate)

where our lines bisect. then part

your perfume sage

honey fiber. ruptured sprawl

last winter. something

extension of snow. of months

the usual postcards of your infant daughters

summer is distant (except for fever and sweating glass)

I recall you at the orchestra hall (primarily interior)

your voice one night. just to say hi.

(the incompatibility of time and tumor)

where have I been? (proximity to you)

fingertips falling. failing

radio silent pulse

still wondering. wandering

where can I reach you beyond the spasmic cling?

Oh, how you closed your eyes.

IN MEMORY OF NAMI. MUSIC ARTERY AND NERVE.

1971–2011

THE ONSET

de-por-tee

部門主義, 分科主義.

de-par-ture [di'pɑ:tʃə; dɪ'pɑrtʃə]
n. ❶離開, 離去。 ❷起程, 出發。 ❸背
離, 變卦。 ❹[航]東西距離, 橫距。

de-pas-ture [di'pɑ:stʃə; dɪ'pæstʃə]
v.i. & i. 食草, 放牧。

de-pend [di'pend; dɪ'pend] v.i. ❶
依賴, 依靠。 ❷信任。 ❸視⋯而定, 遇。
❹懸而未決。

de-pend-a-bil-i-ty [di'pendə'biliti;
ɑɪ,pendə'bɪləti] n. 可靠性, 可依賴。

de-pend-a-ble [di'pendəbl; dɪ'pen-
dəbl] adj. 可靠的, 可依賴的, 可信任的。

de-pend-ence [di'pendəns; dɪ'pen-
dəns] n. ❶依賴, 依靠。 ❷信任。 ❸附
屬, 從屬。

de-pen-den-cy [di'pendənsi; dɪ'pen-
dənsɪ] n. ❶依賴, 信賴。 ❷附屬, 從屬。
❸從屬物。 ❹屬地, 屬國。

de-pen-dent [di'pendənt; dɪ'pend-
ənt] adj. ❶懸垂的。 ❷視⋯而定的。
❸依靠的。 ❹附屬的。 —, n. 依靠者, 侍
從, 眷屬。 [=depopulate.]

de-peo-ple [di:'pi:pl; di'pipəl] v.t.

de-pict [di'pikt; dɪ'pikt] v.t. ❶繪
畫, 描摹。 ❷描寫, 叙述。

de-pic-tion [di'pikʃən; dɪ'pikʃən]
n. ❶繪畫, 描寫, 叙述。 ❷圖畫。

trans-o-ce-an-ic

trans-o-ce-an-ic ['trænzouʃi
'ænik;,trænsoʃi'ænik,,trænz-]*adj*.大洋那
邊的,橫渡大洋的。

tran-som ('trænsəm; 'trænsam] *n*.
❶(門窗的)橫檔,門頂窗。 ❷(車輛的)橫
梁,船尾橫材。

tran-somed ('trænsəmd; 'træn-
səmd] *adj*.(門窗等)附有橫檔的。

trans-pa-cif-ic ('trænspə'sifik;
,trænspə'sıfık] *adj*、橫渡太平洋的,
太平洋那邊的。

trans-pa-dane (træns'peidein;
'trænspə,den, træns'peden] *adj*.
(從羅馬看)Po 河那邊的。

trans-par-ence (træns'peərəns;
træns'perəns] *n*. 透明。

trans-par-en-cy (træns'peərənsi;
træns'perənsi] *n*. ❶透明。 ❷透明
物體。 ❸(照相)透明度。

trans-par-ent (træns'peərənt;
træns'perənt] *adj*. ❶透明的。 ❷坦
白的,明朗的。 ❸顯而易見的。

1   Every year Mother predicts that Ama is going to die.
      Blood is thicker than water, she says, clicking her suitcase shut.

2 *What is my name?* Clinking jade dangles from her spotted wrist, conjures a cool breeze.
  We lean like ships on her shore, under the blue shade of palms.

3   Reach deep into the chasm between the wall and the heavy dresser. Pile the red shoe box with musty faces. There are many of them, incomplete, longing to be filled in.

4   My mother's mother carried everything on the lobes of her ears, sometimes round, milky pearls, other times drops of warm amber. They were heavy like the typhoon rains that bent her in the jungle, just off the shore where the one-way arrived from Jinjiang. Only Buddha had ears as long. Both were blessed with longevity, but only one had the switchblade tongue.

5   *There are no fireworks when girls are born.* My mother is translating her mother.

fa-ther-land

fas-cism [ˈfæʃizm; ˈfæʃ,izəm] *n.* 意
大利的法西斯主義。
fas-cist [ˈfæʃist; ˈfæʃist] *n.* ❶[F-]
法西斯黨員。 ❷法西斯主義者。 —,*adj.*
❶[F-]法西斯黨員的。 ❷法西斯主義的。
Fa-scis-ti [fəˈʃisti, fæˈʃistiː;
fəˈʃisti] *n.* 意大利國粹黨。
fa-scis-tic [fəˈʃistik; fəˈʃistɪk]
adj. =fascist.   「煩悶。」
fash [fæʃ; fæʃ] *v.t. & i.* 困惱, 窘困,
fash-ion [ˈfæʃən; ˈfæʃən] *n.* ❶種
類。 ❷時尚, 樣式, 流行。 ❸製法。 ❹
名流, 上流社會人士。 —,*v.t.* ❶形成, 鑄
造成。 ❷使適合。
fash-ion-a-ble [ˈfæʃnəbl; ˈfæʃənə-
bl] *adj.* ❶時髦的, 流行的。 ❷上流
社會人士愛好的。 —,*n.* 時髦人物。

6   I was almost thirty when diagnosed with acute filial piety.

7   Father taught that to succeed in a new place, one must memorize the dictionary.
     Unable to locate him in the A's, I would go outside to taste the snow.

8   Memories tango, are tangled in plaque fibers of twisted tau. All of us mangled by the
     nothing train that spreads from nerve to nerve. A gliding whisper without brakes.

9   Grandpa read his hand with one swipe of the fingertips along the mahjong tiles'
     facedown bellies. He could smell his nemeses' cigarettes, their dark spice on the
     back of his neck. He touched, calculating the carvings for ones and nines, all four
     winds, that thirteenth orphan. Whatever will free him from this crowded rabble.

10   *You were born a serpent—too unlucky for the gamble.* My father is echoing his father.

mes-ti-zo

'zembri'ænθimən; mes,embri
ænθiməm] *n.* 【植】松葉菊。
mes-en-ter-y ['mesəntəri; 'mesn,
teri] *n.* 【解】腸系膜。
mesh [meʃ; meʃ] *n.* ❶網孔, 篩孔。
❷*pl.* 網, 法網。 ❸【機】齒輪的嚙合。
—*v.t. & v.i.* ❶用網捕。 ❷齒輪嚙合。
me-si-al ['miːziəl, 'mesiəl; 'miziəl,
'mesiəl] *adj.* 中央的, 中間的。
mes-mer-ic[mes'merik,mez'merik;
mes'merik, mez-] *adj.* 催眠
的, 催眠術的。
mes-mer-ism ['mesmərizm, 'mez
mərizm; 'mesmə,rizəm, 'mez-]
n. 催眠術。

11 When a boundary is crossed, the luggage gets lost. To fall asleep, I imagine Little
    Sister sleeping under my blanket.

12 I walk Ama to the rooftop terrace, tiny hand in mine. Her skin is soft and loose
    around the bones, each knuckle adorned with shiny things. Perched by the spider
    plants, Myna, her parrot, is cussing again, telling us uglies to go away.

13   Night is damp. The kitchen light seeps under the guest room door. Never mind both
      heavy lids or the endless buzz of motorbikes below. Just the violent clatter of silver.
      Mother is still feeding her sister.

14   Ghost touching ghost.

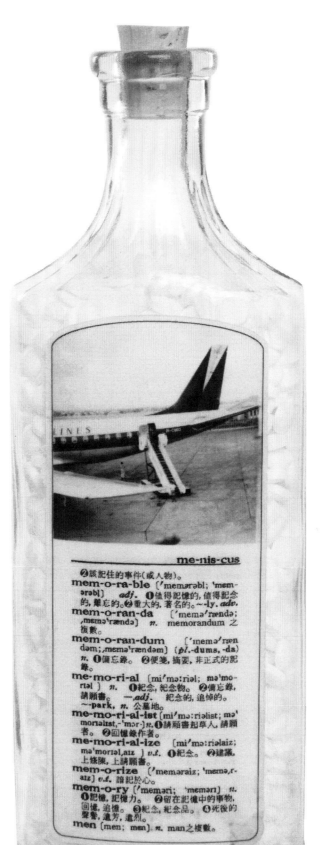

15   We drift in different dictionaries, often hearing each other second hand.
       Her fingertips press upon my simian line the scent of *sampaguitas*.

16 After the sons have all left home, after the inertia of planes, cell mutations, a small chest in its final collapse.

PROFUNDA LINGUAE.

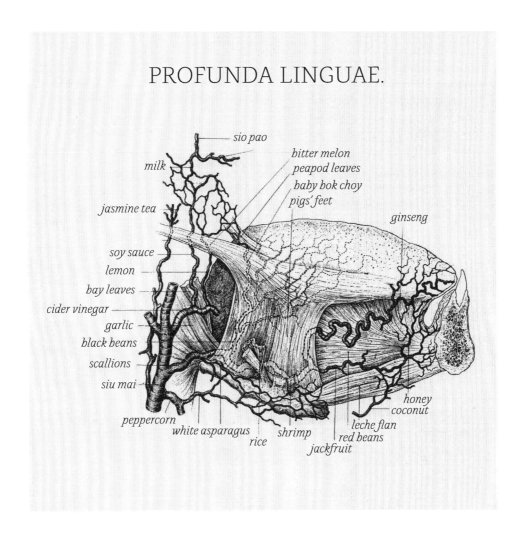

FIG. 1

Father, give me the cure for this midlife heat,
this body taken by fever, sublingual
afraid of never knowing—
    Are you proud?
Hidden under a pillow of bitter melon buds.

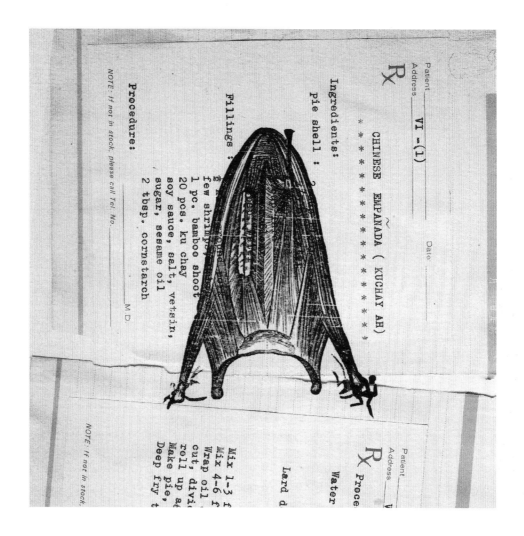

FIG. 2

Do you remember those Sundays,
the rolling clatter of dim sum carts,
so steamy next to the sultry walnut shrimp,
and piquant vegetables who wear anything with
black bean sauce?

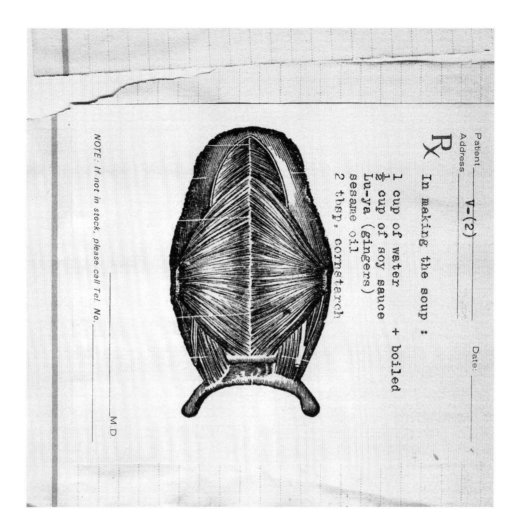

FIG. 3

At the table, we do not speak of ourselves,
never learned the words for *daring* or *disappointed*
don't know how to say
    I feel,
      I'm sorry,
have no idea if you've missed me these last few years.

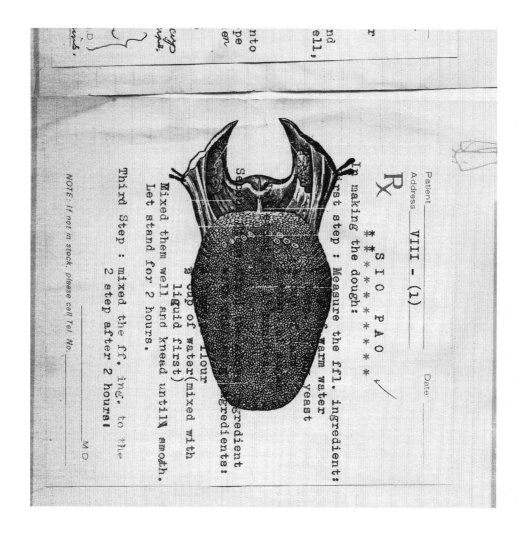

FIG. 4

We know how to agree by suggesting more *sio pao*,
that whatever is left of my piety
I can demonstrate in a perfect pour of tea.
To lighten conversations, the sweet caramel of leche flan.
Halo halo is what we speak, they say—

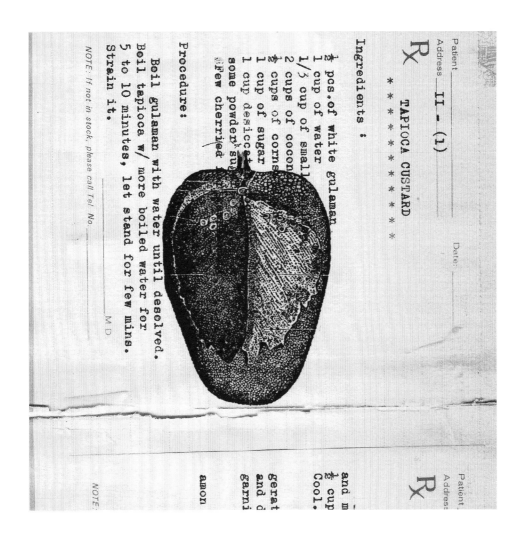

FIG. 5

The dessert of the mestizo soul:
Shaved ice cloaked in the ghost of milk
with layers of yellow jackfruit and red beans,
a purple crown of ube ice cream
topped by clean white coconut.

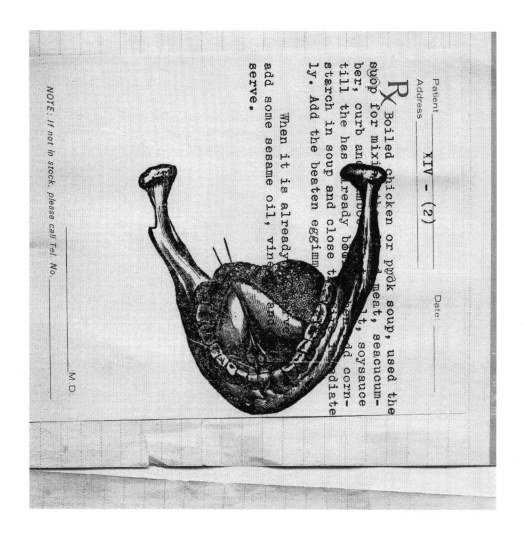

FIG. 6

We taste our selves,
                ripped to shreds—
Though your nerves may be softened or set aflame,
I do not get to see beyond your iron moustache—
Except

74

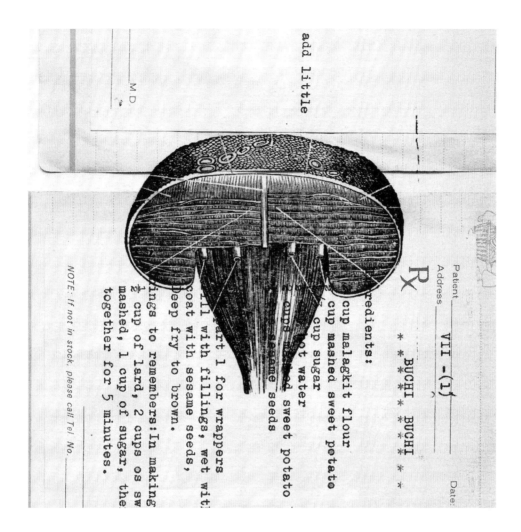

FIG. 7

when you sniff and sniff and sniff,
tending to the silky boil of pigs' feet,
your wrist ladling in concentric circles
the blossom notes of bay leaves with
ginger and garlic cuddling in the gloss of soy.

FIG. 8

The peppercorns, how they crack between my molars
to my palatine pleasure,
hot tang of your quiet devotion,
how it quenches, washes away, leaving a
lump of sugar in my throat.

THE VESSEL.

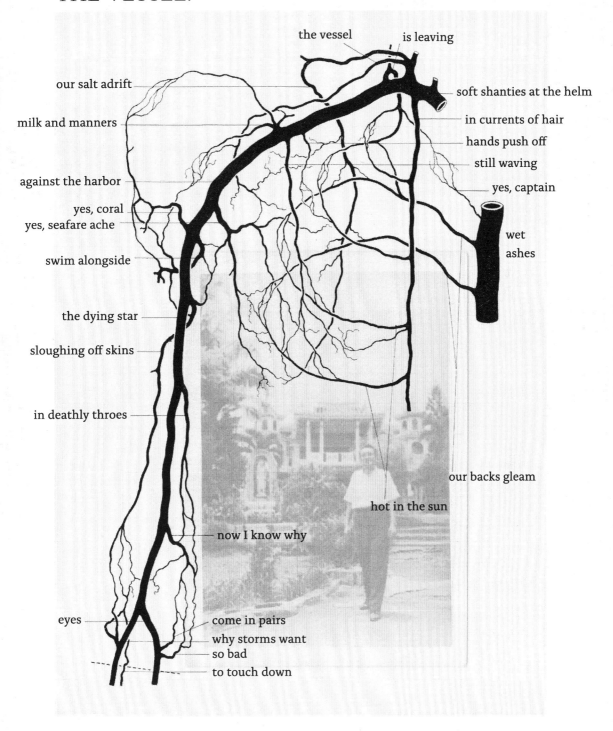

the vessel

is leaving

our salt adrift

soft shanties at the helm

milk and manners

in currents of hair

hands push off

still waving

against the harbor

yes, captain

yes, coral
yes, seafare ache

swim alongside

wet
ashes

the dying star

sloughing off skins

in deathly throes

our backs gleam

hot in the sun

now I know why

eyes

come in pairs

why storms want
so bad

to touch down

THE ATTIC.

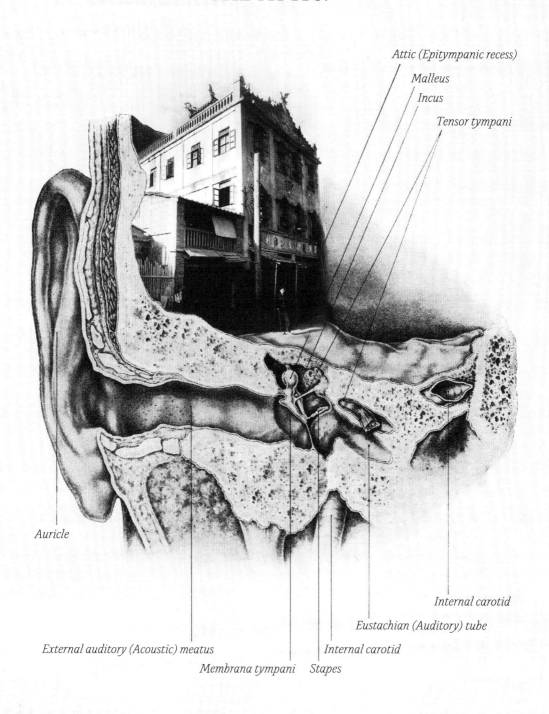

Attic (Epitympanic recess)

Malleus

Incus

Tensor tympani

Auricle

Internal carotid

Eustachian (Auditory) tube

External auditory (Acoustic) meatus

Membrana tympani

Stapes

Internal carotid

ETERNAL AND MIDDLE EAR

By the time you are born, what I know of this world will be well on its way to extinction.
Above your crib, the floorboards creak as I make more room in this attic.

1. *Auricle*

Remember to play games made with ivory or
      shells – I like backgammon and mancala the
      best, the way my fingers brush against my
      mother's hands to pick up all the pieces.
Enjoy the collective clink of sticks on
      corningware, spinning on a lazy susan.
We don't lock doors in this house, and in the
      summers, the windows glow with fireflies.
When I say in the first tone *lai tiah*, it is me
      asking you to bring your warm body to the
      family room, heart within heart.

2. *Membrana tympani*

Do not walk the streets plugging your ears
      with digital waves.
What of the ocean's breath, or the patter of
      tongues that play over mangoes and
      plastic bags?
Perhaps you will be able to feel my father's
      vibrato in your chest, and notice the long
      hair on his adams apple as he sings over
      hissing scallions.
At the table, I will sit with you quietly, not
      looking away even once, until you are done.
      In Hokkien, *tiah* also means to listen.

3. *Malleus*

You will never hear the crackle of landlines,
      how they shroud Ama's voice like a fishing
      boat in the mouth of a monsoon, as she
      mourns Grandpa's fate in the shark-
      infested waters.
There are no schools to teach you the diction
      of our kin who fled.
These eyes can't even make out the markings.
When we say it in the fourth tone,
tiah is the word for ache.

4. *Internal carotid*

Go. Go to the countries that have not yet
      been named.
No need to hum like me on my sewing
      machine, for I have already embroidered
      my story in blood.
There will be a larger hum, beckoning you
      beyond the laurel trees, through door upon
      open door, towards cranes that climb
      endlessly up the sky.
At night, I will thumb my red spool of thread
      and tug at you, mend your tears,
      whisper while you are sleeping:
      Gua tzin tiah di, my child, for
      tiah is the other name for love.

Notes

Hokkien is a southern Chinese dialect spoken by overseas Chinese in the Philippines. *Mandarin* is the official language of China. *Tagalog* is the official language of the Philippines.

Epigraph: Susan Howe, "Statement for the New Poetics Colloquium, Vancouver, 1985," Jimmy and Lucy's House of 'K', 5 (November 1985):

1. "The Glass Larynx": The text on the right side is from "Action and Non-Action" by Chuang Tzu, translated by Thomas Merton, from *The Way Of Chuang Tzu*, copyright ©1965 by The Abbey of Gethsemani. Reprinted by permission of New Directions Publishing Corp. Chuang Tzu 莊子 (b. 369 BC) was a Chinese philosopher and poet whose writings were influential to Taoism. My family shares the same Chinese surname as Chuang 莊 with my generation being the 25th.

4. "Paper Son": Xiamen 下門 is a port city in the southeast province of Fujian, China. Its name was later changed to 廈門, which is pronounced the same way but means "gate to the mansion." Xiamen is also my paternal grandmother's birthplace. Luzon is the northern region of the Philippines where Manila is located. *Intsik* is slang that refers to Chinese people, and in some contexts considered a derogatory term. *Pulis* is tagalog for police. My paternal grandfather fled to the Philippines in 1938, entering on purchased papers belonging to a deceased person. He assumed the surname Ong on legal documents, but also retained his Chinese name.

5. "Corona Mestiza": *Amoy* refers to people from the Xiamen region of Fujian. *Pinoy* is an informal term for Filipino people. *Mestizo* describes persons of mixed heritage.

6. "Fortune Babies": There is some family folklore surrounding my Uncle Se-Ahn's adoption. One version is rooted in the belief that couples having difficulty conceiving sons should adopt a boy in order to attract more "lucky" fertility. Uncle Se-Ahn was not known to me until my early adulthood, which is when we visited him in China.

8. "Catching a Wave": Due to the gender preference for boys in China and other Asian countries, ultrasound machines have been banned in some places for gender determination. The practice of aborting baby girls has altered the gender balance such that there are approximately 124 boys to every 100 girls. *Bare branches* is the term for male bachelors, for which there is an overabundance. Some estimate the disappearance of baby girls at 100 million or higher. ("The War on Baby Girls: Gendercide," *The Economist*, March 4, 2010, URL: www.economist.com/node/15606229)

16. "Medica Visits the Witch Doctor": *Tsinelas* is tagalog for sandals. *Mangkukulam* is tagalog for a sorcerer or witch who practices black magic.

18. "Whitening Solution": "If you have white skin, you can cover 1,000 uglinesses." This saying is quoted by a young woman in an article about Asian American women pursuing whiter skin despite health risks. ("Beauty and the Bleach" by Ja-Rui Chong, *Los Angeles Times*, July 26, 2005, URL: articles.latimes.com/2005/jul/26/local/me-whitening26)

20. "Oral Whitening Rinse": "Truthful words are not beautiful, beautiful words are not truthful." This Chinese paradox is often attributed to Lao Tzu, the Taoist philosopher and author of the *Tao Te Ching*.

23. "Metal Lungs": *Po* 魄 refers to the soul of the body. *Qi* 氣 refers to life force.

35. "Innervation": Quoted here are my mother's sayings. *One eye open, one eye closed*: her secret to longevity in marriage. *Blood is thicker than water*: her admonition to stay close to family. *You have to collect and select*: her dating advice.

36. "Silent Treatment": *Spiritos* refers to spirits that enter and possess a person's body.

40. "Etymology of an Untranslated Cervix": The epigraph is from an online article "Cervical Cancer in Uganda" on the website of Prevention International: No Cervical Cancer, authored by Erin Cox, MD, April 3, 2010. (www.pincc.org/campaigns/cervical-cancer-uganda-stats-and-more-glimpse-our-project)

43. "The Onset": *Sampaguita* is the name for the Arabian jasmine flower, which is also the national flower of the Philippines. *Ama* is a Hokkien title for Grandmother. Jinjiang 晉江, a town located in the Fujian province, is the birthplace of my maternal grandmother.

69. "Profunda Linguae": *Halo halo* is tagalog for "mixed together" and refers to one of my father's favorite Filipino desserts. The base is shaved ice and condensed milk layered with a rainbow of various toppings including red beans, jello, fruit, and ice cream.

81. "The Attic": *Mancala* refers to a popular "sowing" board game that is played on a wooden board with rows of holes. *Guah tzin tiah di* is Hokkien for "I truly love you."

Illustrations

Title page: Illustration of anastomoses of arteries around the scapula from *Surgical Anatomy* by John B. Deaver, published by P. Blackinton's Son & Co, Philadelphia, 1899.

1. "The Glass Larynx": Anatomical illustration of the larynx from *Surgical Anatomy* by John B. Deaver, published by P. Blackinton's Son & Co, Philadelphia, 1899.

2. "Bo Suerte": Digital collage titled *Mother as a Boy* (2001) based on a photo of my mother and her siblings with one of their "aunties" in Manila. My mother is the boy who is standing second in from the right.

5. "Corona Mestiza": Digital collage made from a found brain scan and map of the Philippine islands.

6. "Fortune Babies": Medicine bottle based on a portrait (c. 1940) of my grandparents with the boy they adopted, named Se-Ahn. He lived with my mother's family until his early adult years when he returned to China.

8. "Catching a Wave": This series of images are from ultrasounds scans taken during my pregnancy as well as my sister's.

14. "Perfect Baby Formula": This is a found image of a newborn that was sent to my grandparents by a family friend. The boy is pictured without pants as a way of providing undisputed evidence of his male gender. This may have been a social response to the way girls were being disguised as boys in family portraits, as my grandfather did.

16. "Medica Visits the Witch Doctor": Found image of Chinese acupuncture chart.

18, 20. "Whitening Solution" & "Oral Whitening Rinse": Found family photos.

23. "Metal Lungs": Illustration of the lung from *Surgical Anatomy* by John B. Deaver, published in 1899. The following sequence of images are sourced from found medical ephemera and family photos.

35. "Innervation": Collage with diagram of the lower intercostal nerve from *Surgical Anatomy* by John B. Deaver, 1926 edition, and found family photos.

36, 38. "Silent Treatment" & "Her Youth in Asia": Photos of my maternal aunt as a girl.

41. "Etymology of an Untranslated Cervix": Collage based on a found medical scan and original photography.

42. "Elegy": This illustration of the deep vessels of the forearm comes from a 1926 edition of *Surgical Anatomy* by John B. Deaver.

43. "The Onset": All the images are based on family photos. *Withstood*: my mother's grandmother. *Patriarchy*: my maternal grandfather. *Hers*: my paternal aunt Asunción as a young girl. *Mutable*: my father as a boy. *Mestizo*: my father as a young man with nieces and nephews. *Tranquilize*: my mother. *Pilgrimage*: my paternal grandfather's home in Manila. The entries are portions of a vintage Chinese-English dictionary.

69. "Profunda Linguae": *Fig 1*: Illustration of the arteries of the tongue from *Surgical Anatomy* by John B. Deaver, 1926 edition. *Fig 2-7*: Scans of favorite Chinese-Filipino recipes my mother typed onto my father's prescription pads, then taped into a notebook, an act of homesickness after her arrival to the United States during the mid-1970's. Layered onto the recipes are anatomical views of the tongue, which come from a 1908 Edwardian chart. *Fig 8*. Portrait of my father.

79. "The Vessel": Collage with illustration of collateral circulation from *Surgical Anatomy* by John B. Deaver, published in 1899. Includes family photograph of my maternal grandfather.

80. "The Attic": Collage with illustration of the external and middle ear from *Surgical Anatomy* by John B. Deaver, 1926 edition. Includes family photograph of my paternal grandfather in front of his home in the Philippines.

All medicine bottles depicted in this collection are archival prints on paper installed on vintage medicine bottles with epoxy and varnish. Photographed by Steffen Allen.

Acknowledgments

These works have appeared in the following publications:

Seneca Review. Beyond Categories Issue. (2014) "Profunda Linguae," "The Attic," "Medica Visits the Witch Doctor."

Loaded Bicycle. Issue 2.1. (2013) "Catching a Wave."

Glassworks Magazine. Issue 6. (2013) "Innervation."

Tidal Basin Review. Featured artist. (2012) "Bo Suerte," "Perfect Baby Formula," "Silent Treatment," "Old Timer's Dis-ease," "Oral Whitening Rinse," "Whitening Solution."

Drunken Boat. Issue 15. (2012) "Metal Lungs."

The New Sound Interdisciplinary Journal of Literature and Art. Issue 1. (2012) "Elegy."

Lantern Review. (2011) "Corona Mestiza."

Special Thanks

Thank you to Joy Harjo for selecting *Silent Anatomies* as the winner of the 2014 Kore Press First Book Award in poetry. I'm grateful to Lisa Bowden and Kore Press for publishing this collection and their commitment to women in literature. Thank you Helen Schaefer and Eva Harris for your support to help make this First Book Award publication possible.

This would not have been possible without the encouragement of my Kundiman family. I am indebted to Sarah Gambito and Joseph Legaspi for the founding of this vital creative home. Thank you to Wendy S. Walters and Randall Horton for your mentorship. Thank you to Douglas Kearney, Rick Barot, Éireann Lorsung, and Dong Li for your wondrous support. Thanks to WomanMade Gallery in Chicago, The Poetry Institute of New Haven, First Person Plural in Harlem, the Kenyon Review Writer's Workshop on Literary Hybrid/ Book Arts, and the Vermont Studio Center for giving this work space to flourish.

Deep thanks to my life mentor, Daisaku Ikeda, and to Nichiren Daishonin and Shakyamuni for helping me discover the treasures of the heart. Thank you to Yuko Nagai, Brad Larsen Sanchez, and the rest of my SGI family for your lifelong embrace.

This collection is in honor of my devoted parents Alejandro and Gloria, my siblings Emmelyn and Chester, as well as our ancestors who risked everything for us. I am deeply grateful to my aunties, uncles, and cousins for helping me to remember *home*. To Kay, Harry, and my wonderful Parker, thank you for making this life so sweet. Finally, thanks to my husband, Andrew, for always supporting my dreams and for bringing a healthy dose of laughter to our creative journey together.

What fortune, what joy.

About the Author

Monica Ong is a visual artist and poet based in Connecticut. Her work has been published in journals such as the *Lantern Review, Drunken Boat, Glassworks Magazine, Loaded Bicycle, Tidal Basin Review,* and the *Seneca Review.* She completed her MFA in Digital Media at the Rhode Island School of Design and is also a Kundiman poetry fellow.

© MATTHEW FRIED

Kore Press

 Kore Press has been standing by women's words since 1993. We are a community of literary activists committed to bringing forth a diversity of women's voices through works that meet the highest artistic standards, and so publish the creative genius of all women writers to deepen awareness and advance social justice.

Since its inception in 1923, *Time Magazine* has had one female editor.

Since 1948, the Pulitzer Prize for Fiction has gone to 42 men and 17 women.

26% of the members of *The New York Times* editorial board are women, 35% at *The Wallstreet Journal*, and 33% at the *Los Angeles Times*

To support feminist publishing—and help lift up "half the sky" as a way to create long-term, sustainable change and a luminous future for all—you can purchase a Kore Press book directly from the publisher, make a tax-deductible gift to the vital production of contemporary literature by women, or become a member of the Press online at www.korepress.org.